Reading Essentials® in Science

HUMAN BODY BASICS

Skin

CHRISTINE WEBSTER

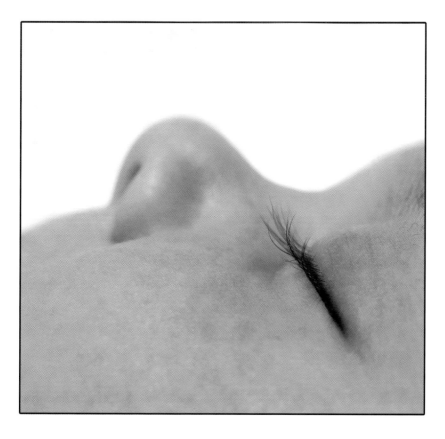

PERFECTION LEARNING®

Editorial Director:	Susan C. Thies
Editor:	Mary L. Bush
Design Director:	Randy Messer
Book Designer:	Mark Hagenberg
Cover Designer:	Michael A. Aspengren
Photo Researcher:	Lisa Leatherman

A special thanks to the following for his scientific review of the book:
Paul Pistek, Instructor of Biological Sciences, North Iowa Area
Community College

Dedication
To my husband Duane—for everything

Image credits
© Dung Vo Trung/CORBIS SYGMA: p. 17; © Lester V. Bergman/CORBIS: p. 8 (bottom);
© Stephanie Sinclair/CORBIS: p. 16; Getty (Rights-Managed): pp. 10 (bottom), 13, 20;
Schering Plough Consumer Health Care: p. 21

iStockphoto: pp. 10 (top, center), 11, 14 (bottom), 18 (bottom), 19 (bottom);
LifeArt: pp. 12 (left), 15, 19 (top); Photos.com: cover, pp. 3, 4, 5, 6, 7, 8 (top), 9, 12 (right),
14 (top), 18 (top), 24

For information, contact
Perfection Learning® Corporation
1000 North Second Avenue, P.O. Box 500
Logan, Iowa 51546-0500.
Phone: 1-800-831-4190
Fax: 1-800-543-2745
perfectionlearning.com

1 2 3 4 5 6 PP 10 09 08 07 06 05

Paperback ISBN 0-7891-6632-1
Reinforced Library Binding ISBN 0-7569-4692-1

Table of Contents

CHAPTER ONE

Skin—It Has You Covered!

Do you know what your largest body **organ** is? You might be thinking your brain or your heart or maybe even your lungs. But none of those is correct. Here's a hint—this organ covers every inch of your body. That's right, it's your skin!

Skin is the outer covering of a body. It's made of layers of **cells** that are stacked on top of one another. Altogether, these layers are about $1/2$ to 4 millimeters thick. The thickest skin is found on the palms of the hands and the bottoms of the feet. The thinnest skin is found on the eyelids.

An adult has about 20 square feet of skin. If you spread it out, that's about the size of a blanket.

An adult's skin weighs about 9 pounds. That's not much compared to the weight of the rest of the body, but it is a lot compared to the weight of other organs. The brain, for example, only weighs 3 pounds. The heart only weighs 9 to 11 ounces.

A Very Busy Organ

Your heart beats and your lungs pump air in and out. What does your skin do? Although skin doesn't appear to *do* anything, it actually does a lot for you. Skin is like the wrapping on a package. It holds everything in and protects it from harm.

Without skin, your insides would be exposed to the big, bad world. Dust, dirt, and germs could attack your other organs easily. Skin acts as a defensive shield against these harmful invaders.

Inquire and Investigate | *The Skin as a Protector*

Question: How does the skin keep germs out of the body?

Answer the question: I think that skin keeps germs out of the body by _____.

Form a hypothesis: Skin keeps germs out of the body by _____

_____.

Test the hypothesis:

Materials
2 oranges with
   undamaged skin
2 small plastic bags
   that seal
dry soil
spoon
pencil

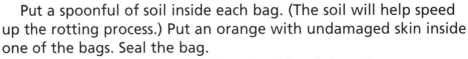

Procedure

Put a spoonful of soil inside each bag. (The soil will help speed up the rotting process.) Put an orange with undamaged skin inside one of the bags. Seal the bag.

With the spoon or pencil, injure the skin of the other orange. Puncture it, scrape it, or bruise it. Place this injured orange in the other bag and seal it.

Put the two bags in a safe spot. Predict what might happen to each orange. Record your predictions. Check the oranges in a few days. What's happening? Record your findings. After a week, compare the injured orange to the uninjured one. Record your observations.

Observations: The orange with the damaged skin rotted faster than the one with the uninjured skin.

Conclusions: Skin keeps germs out of the body by forming a protective seal around the outside. When the skin is broken or damaged, the seal is broken and dirt and bacteria can get inside and cause infection and illness.

Skin acts as a sunshade for your body. It blocks the Sun's powerful rays from reaching your other organs and body parts.

The skin also houses the **nerve cells** that allow you to feel temperature, pressure, pain, and other sensations. When you touch something, these nerve cells spring into action and report the feeling to your brain or spinal cord.

Teamwork

Healthy bones and teeth depend on skin. With the help of sunlight, the skin produces vitamin D. Vitamin D helps a body absorb calcium, which makes bones and teeth hard and strong.

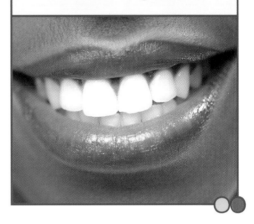

Wrap It Up!

Skin is like your own personal wrapping paper. No one else has exactly the same skin as you do. Its color and texture are designed just for you. Even your freckles and wrinkles (or lack of them) are unique. Your skin puts a perfect finish on a great inside package!

CHAPTER TWO

A Look at the Layers

Skin has two main layers. They are the **epidermis** and the **dermis**. Each layer has its own responsibilities in the body.

Magnified skin tissue of a finger

On the Surface: The Epidermis

The epidermis is the outer layer of skin that you see every time you look in the mirror. This tough, waterproof layer is about as thick as a sheet of paper.

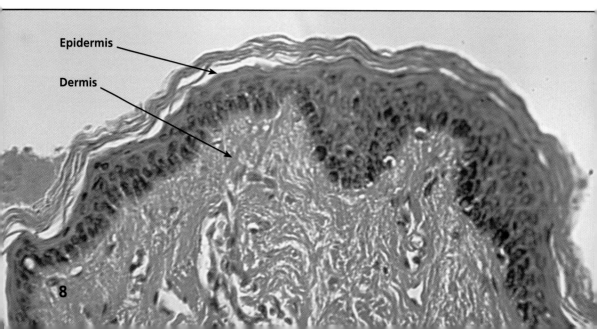

Epidermis

Dermis

The epidermis is actually made up of many layers of cells that are slowly moving to the surface of the skin. New cells are constantly being produced at the bottom. These new cells push older cells to the top. As the older cells move upward, they produce **keratin**. Keratin is a tough material that makes skin strong and waterproof. By the time these keratin-filled cells reach the surface, they are dead and flattened. This process takes about a month.

Not Just for Skin

The nails on your fingers and toes are also made of hardened keratin. Animal hooves, horns, feathers, and hair (fur) also contain keratin.

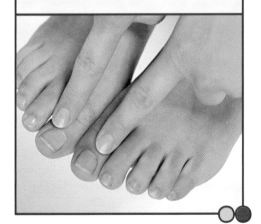

Eventually the top layer of dead skin cells rubs or flakes off. In fact, humans lose about 30,000 to 40,000 dead skin cells each minute. As skin cells are lost, a new layer of cells moves up to replace them. These dead cells make up a large part of the dust in your house.

Another important material produced in the epidermis is **melanin**. Melanin is a **pigment** that gives skin its color. People with dark skin have cells that produce a lot of melanin. People with lighter skin have cells that produce less melanin.

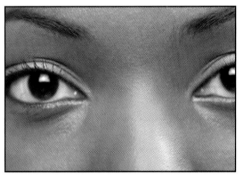

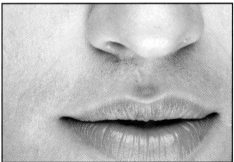

Melanin protects the skin from the Sun's harmful rays. People with dark skin tend to get sunburned less than those with lighter skin.

Melanin is also the cause of suntans and freckles. When skin is exposed to sunlight, more melanin is produced. This causes a darkening of the skin known as a suntan. A suntan fades when the skin cells with extra melanin are rubbed off.

Freckles are dark spots on the skin caused by clusters of extra melanin. They are more common in people with lighter skin. Being out in the Sun can cause freckles or make existing ones darker. Sometimes freckles fade with less exposure to the Sun.

White Without Melanin

A few people have skin cells that don't produce melanin. This is called *albinism*. Albinos have very white skin that is easily burned by the Sun.

If you look at your fingertips, you'll see tiny swirling lines. If you press your fingers or thumbs on a pad of ink and then on paper, these lines will show up clearly in your fingerprints. Fingerprints are patterns of ridges on the skin of your fingers. They were formed as skin cell layers developed before you were born. No one's fingerprints are exactly the same—not even twins. This is why they can be used to identify people.

Beneath the Surface: The Dermis

The bottom layer of the skin is known as the dermis. There's a lot of action going on in this layer.

Blood vessels in the dermis deliver oxygen and **nutrients** to the skin. This nourishes the dermis so the cells stay healthy and continue to **reproduce**. The epidermis doesn't have its own blood supply, so the dermis supports it too.

One of the dermis's jobs is to keep a person's body temperature comfortable—not too hot or too cold. Sweat **glands** in the dermis keep a body cool. These glands produce the salty fluid called *sweat*. When a body gets too hot, the glands release sweat through **pores**, or holes, in the skin. When the sweat **evaporates** into the air, it takes heat with it. When a body is too cold, the blood vessels in the skin get narrower to keep in heat.

Another Job for Sweat

Sweat glands also help a body get rid of waste. A small amount of certain materials that a body doesn't need are carried out of the body by sweat.

11

Hair growth begins in the dermis. Each piece of hair grows from a tube called a *follicle*. The hair grows and travels up through the dermis and out the epidermis. You have hair follicles over most of your body, except for areas like your lips, palms, and bottoms of your feet. You have more than 100,000 hair follicles on just your head!

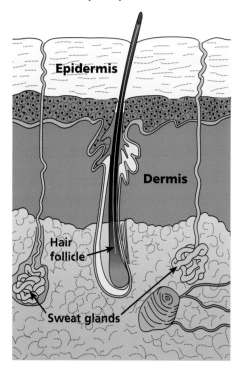

Epidermis

Dermis

Hair follicle

Sweat glands

The sebaceous glands are found in the dermis. These glands produce an oil called *sebum*. Sebum keeps skin and hair soft and shiny. It also makes your skin waterproof. Sebaceous glands are commonly found in skin with hair. Hairless areas of the body may or may not have these glands. There are no sebaceous glands, for example, on the palms of the hands or the bottoms of the feet.

The dermis also contains a material called **collagen**. Collagen adds to skin's incredible strength.

Has your mom ever told you to stop making silly faces or your face will freeze that way? That's not true, thanks to the dermis. The dermis is responsible for the skin's ability to stretch and return to normal. This is called *elasticity*. As you age, your skin loses some of its elasticity. This results in wrinkles.

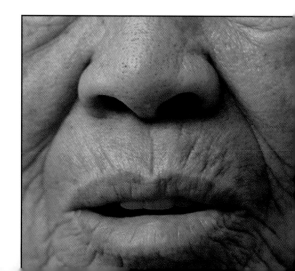

Imagine what would happen if you touched something hot on the stove and couldn't feel it. The nerve cells in the dermis make sure this doesn't happen. These cells pick up feelings such as temperature, pain, and texture. They send messages about these feelings to your brain or spinal cord. Then your brain or spinal cord tells you what you feel.

Getting Under Your Skin

Underneath the dermis is the **subcutaneous layer**. This layer is made of connective and fatty **tissues**. The loose connective tissue joins the skin to other body parts such as bones and muscles. Without this tissue, your skin would just be floating on top of your body.

The fatty tissue keeps your body warm. It also provides a cushion when you fall down or bang yourself on something. About half of a person's body fat is found in the subcutaneous layer. It can be more than an inch thick in certain areas of your body.

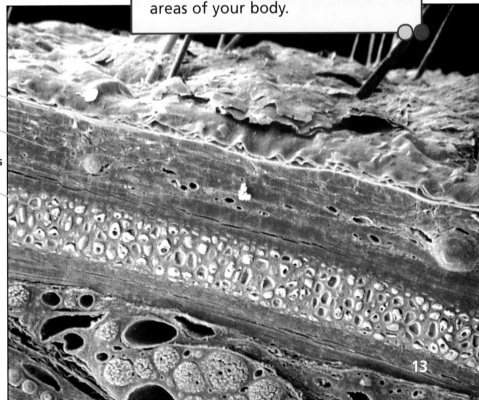

Epidermis

Dermis

Subcutaneous layer

CHAPTER THREE

Injury and Repair

Remember when you were a little kid and your knees were scraped up all summer long? Even though your skin is strong, it can't protect you from everything. Scrapes, scratches, cuts, and burns are part of a skin's life. Luckily, skin can usually repair itself, supplying you with new skin that's as good as the old.

Cut It Out

Ouch! A scrape or cut can hurt. But usually these types of injuries heal fast and a new layer of skin replaces the wounded one.

A simple scrape normally involves just the outer layer of skin. The epidermis can quickly and easily repair itself. The scraping of the skin and the loss of skin cells trigger the skin's replacement process. Cells along the scraped area begin to divide to fill in the gap. This healing often takes just a few days.

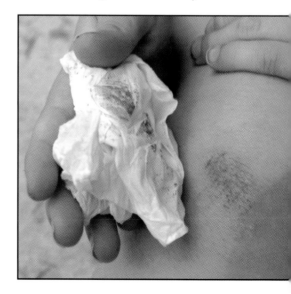

A deeper wound involves both layers of skin. When blood vessels in the dermis are cut, there's bleeding. After the blood **clots** and forms a scab, the skin cells start moving in. They get busy forming a sheet of new cells over the wound. Some of these cells deposit collagen into the wound to help repair the dermis. This collagen fills in the gaps in the skin where the cut occurred. When the wound heals, the extra collagen may form a scar.

Burning Up

Burns are another type of skin injury. Some burns are minor. Everyone has burned a finger on something hot at least once in his or her lifetime. Other burns can be life-threatening. When large areas of a person's body are seriously burned, the body can't control its temperature. Body fluids may be lost, and infection can set in. Being without healthy skin can be deadly.

There are three types of burns. First-degree burns only affect the epidermis. An example of this is a mild sunburn. Second-degree burns affect the entire epidermis and some of the dermis. These burns are painful and usually cause blistering. You can get these types of burns from touching a hot oven. Third-degree burns destroy the epidermis and seriously damage (or destroy) the dermis all the way down to the subcutaneous layer. Many burns from fires are third-degree burns.

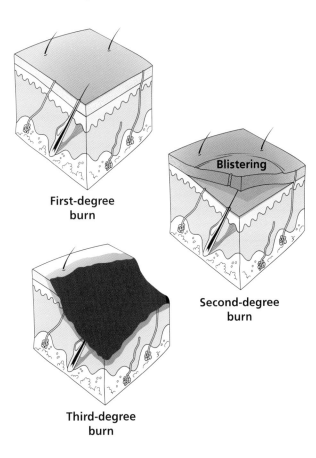

First-degree burn

Blistering

Second-degree burn

Third-degree burn

The skin can usually repair itself after first- and second-degree burns. New skin cells grow and replace the burned ones. However, when skin is completely destroyed, there are no cells left to produce new cells and the skin is dead. This is where the amazing technology of a skin graft can help. A skin graft uses healthy skin to help repair burned skin. Skin is taken from an undamaged area on the body (or from another person). The piece of skin is grafted, or moved, to the burned area. Blood vessels from the surrounding area move into the grafted skin. The grafted skin begins to grow and produce new skin cells to replace the lost ones. Eventually the skin graft heals and connects with the rest of the body's skin.

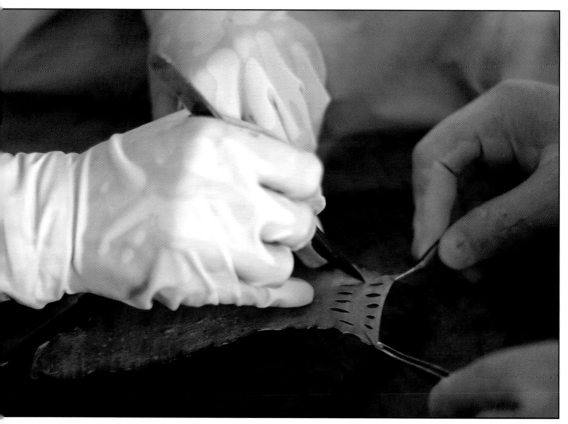

Doctors prepare skin taken from one leg of a patient. The healthy skin will then be grafted onto the other leg, which was severely burned.

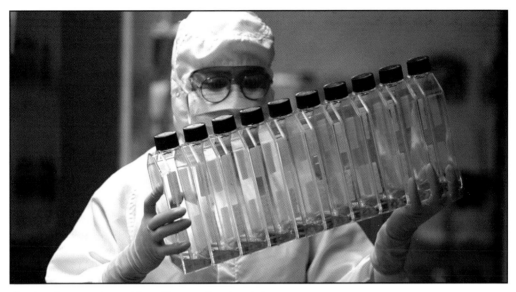

A scientist examines skin cells growing in a lab.

Sometimes a burn is just too big, and there isn't enough healthy skin available to use for a graft. Luckily, scientists have made an amazing advance in skin technology called *tissue engineering*. This technique has saved the lives of many burn victims.

In tissue engineering, a small piece of undamaged skin is removed from a burn patient's body. The tissue is then sent to a lab. Here, nutrients are added to the skin, and the cells start to multiply. Large sheets of skin cells grow in just a few weeks. The new skin sheets are then transferred to the burned areas on the patient. Eventually the sheets grow together into one new covering of skin.

The new skin isn't exactly like natural skin. It doesn't have sweat glands, hair follicles, or normal amounts of melanin. It does, however, provide burn victims with the protective covering they need to survive. Eventually, the body can start to re-create some of skin's natural properties.

CHAPTER FOUR

Taking Care of Your Skin

Your skin is one of your best protectors, but it's also up to *you* to protect *it*. Skin can get overactive or irritated. Other times serious illness can attack. Taking care of your skin is the number one way to protect it and keep it healthy.

Acne

Acne is an annoying skin condition that anyone can get. It is most common, however, among teenagers. This is because teenage bodies produce more oil (sebum) than usual. The extra oil can block pores in the skin.

The blocked pores form bumps on the skin called *pimples*.

Keeping your skin clean will help prevent acne. Washing your face with a mild soap and water several times a day will keep oil from building up in your pores.

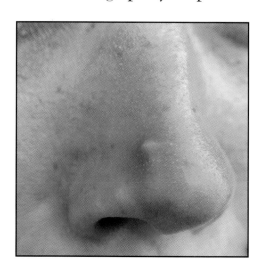

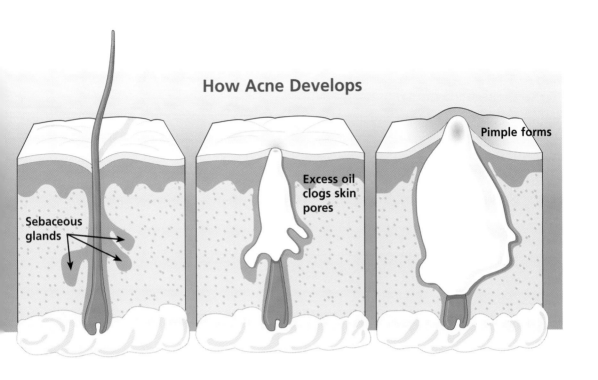

How Acne Develops

Sebaceous glands

Excess oil clogs skin pores

Pimple forms

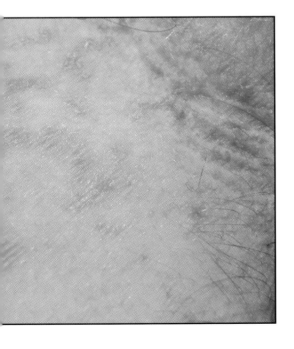

Dermatitis

Dermatitis is a skin condition that may cause dryness, itching, and redness. There are different types of dermatitis. Some are caused by **allergies**. Others are caused when the skin comes in contact with something that irritates it, such as poison ivy or detergents. Avoiding irritating objects and using soothing creams can help relieve dermatitis.

Skin Cancer

Skin cancer is a disease that causes abnormal skin cells to spread quickly, overtaking healthy cells. If left alone, the abnormal cells can spread throughout the body and become deadly.

The Sun is a major factor in the cause of skin cancer. The Sun's harmful rays can damage skin cells. These damaged cells can turn into cancer. To prevent this, cover your body with as much clothing as possible, including a hat, when out in the Sun. Always put sunscreen on any areas of your skin that aren't covered. Sunscreen blocks the Sun's dangerous rays from reaching your skin.

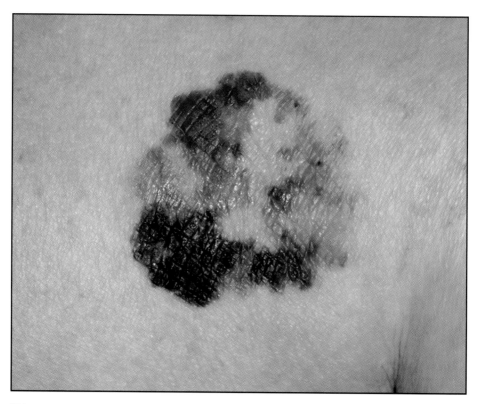

Skin cancer

In the early 1900s, several scientists tried to create a sunscreen that worked. In 1944, Benjamin Green finally got it right. During World War II, Green began to worry about the soldiers who were outside all day. Many were getting sunburned. He decided to invent something to help protect them. Green experimented in his kitchen. He cooked cocoa butter and other ingredients. Then he tried each batch of sunscreen on his own bald head. Finally, he came up with a combination that worked.

Green began selling his sunscreen cream. Soon he started his own company to make and sell his products. He called the company Coppertone. Coppertone has since made many improvements on Green's sunscreen and other sun-protection products.

It Really Does Have You Covered!

Your skin protects you every day. It's your responsibility to keep your skin clean and healthy. If you take care of your skin, it will keep you covered for life.

21

Internet Connections and Related Reading for Skin

http://kidshealth.org/kid/body/skin_noSW.html
Get the whole story on skin at this KidsHealth site.

http://yucky.kids.discovery.com/noflash/body/pg000146.html
Check out these gross and cool facts about your skin.

http://www.bbc.co.uk/health/kids/skin.shtml
Find out how the skin matters to your body.

http://www.geocities.com/Athens/Atrium/5924/fingerprintingbackground.htm
What type of fingerprints do you have? This interesting student site on fingerprints will help you decide.

Skin by Tracy Maurer. A Bodyworks book on skin. Rourke Book Company, Inc., 1999. ISBN 0-8659-3582-3. [RL 4 IL 1–4] (3808006 HB)

Your Skin and Mine by Paul Showers. From freckles to fingerprints to follicles, learn all about skin—what it is and how it protects you. HarperCollins, 1991. ISBN 0-0644-5102-4 (PB) 0-0602-2522-x (CC). [RL 3 IL K–3] (8746501 PB 8746502 CC)

•RL = Reading Level
•IL = Interest Level
Perfection Learning's catalog numbers are included
for your ordering convenience. PB indicates paperback.
CC indicates Cover Craft. HB indicates hardback.

Glossary

allergy (AL er jee) unusual sensitivity to a normally harmless substance

blood vessel (bluhd VES uhl) tube that carries blood around the body

cell (sel) smallest unit of living matter

clot (klaht) to thicken and form lumps

collagen (KAHL uh jin) strong material found in skin, bones, and other connective tissues (see separate entry for *tissue*)

dermis (DER mis) bottom layer of skin

epidermis (ep uh DER mis) surface layer of skin

evaporate (ee VAP or ayt) to change from a liquid to a gas

gland (gland) organ or group of cells that produces and releases substances that the body needs (see separate entries for *organ* and *cell*)

keratin (KAIR uh tin) substance in the skin that makes it tough

melanin (MEL uh nuhn) pigment in the skin that gives it its color (see separate entry for *pigment*)

nerve cell (nerv sel) cell that sends messages around the body (see separate entry for *cell*)

nutrient (NOO tree ent) material that living things need to stay healthy and grow

organ (OR guhn) part of the body such as the skin, heart, or lungs

pigment (PIG ment) substance that gives something its color

pore (por) tiny opening in the human skin

reproduce (ree pruh DOOS) to make more

subcutaneous layer (suhb kyou TAY nee uhs LAY er) layer of connective and fatty tissues beneath the skin (see separate entry for *tissue*)

tissue (TISH you) group of similar cells that work together to perform a job in the body

Index